WORKBOOK

FOR

NEVER SPLIT THE DIFFERENCE

An Implementation Guide To Chris Voss's Book: Negotiating As If Your Life Depended On It

MEMORIES PRINTS

This Book Belongs To

DISCLAIMER:

This workbook's material and recommendations are provided solely for your convenience and are not a replacement for expert guidance.

The workbook's author and publisher expressly disclaim all liability and responsibility for any loss or harm that may be attributable to any advice or material in the workbook.

HOW TO USE THIS WORKBOOK

1. Begin with the Book:
Start by reading or reviewing "Never Split the Difference" by Chris Voss. Familiarize yourself with the key concepts and strategies presented in the book.

2. Chapter Summaries:
Refer to the workbook's chapter summaries to refresh your memory on the main ideas from each section. Use this as a quick reference guide before diving into the workbook exercises.

3. Engage with Exercises:
Complete the practical exercises provided in each section of the workbook. These activities are designed to help you internalize the negotiation principles and apply them to real-world scenarios. Consider engaging in role-playing, case studies, or self-reflection exercises to reinforce your learning.

4. Reflection Questions:
Pause and reflect on the thought-provoking questions at the end of each chapter. Take the time to consider how the principles discussed relate to your own experiences and how you can incorporate them into your negotiation style.

5. Real-world Application:

Apply the learned principles to your daily life. Whether negotiating a business deal, navigating personal relationships, or making significant life decisions, use the workbook as a guide to implementing the strategies advocated by Chris Voss.

6. Track Your Progress:

Keep track of your progress throughout the workbook. Note areas where you feel more confident and identify those that may require additional practice. Use the workbook as a tool for continuous improvement in your negotiation skills.

7. Seek Feedback:

Consider discussing your workbook experience with peers or mentors. Share your insights, challenges, and successes. External perspectives can provide valuable feedback and enhance your understanding of the negotiation principles.

8. Apply and Adapt:

Negotiation is a dynamic skill that evolves with practice. Apply the principles consistently, adapt them to different situations, and refine your approach based on the feedback and outcomes you experience.

By actively engaging with the workbook, you'll transform theoretical knowledge into practical skills, becoming a more effective and confident negotiator in various aspects of your life. Remember, the key to mastering negotiation is continuous learning and application. Enjoy your journey to mastering the art of negotiation!

OVERVIEW

Welcome to the interactive workbook designed to accompany the gripping insights of Chris Voss's "Never Split the Difference: Negotiating As If Your Life Depended On It." As a former international hostage negotiator for the FBI, Voss's unique perspective on high-stakes negotiations takes us deep into the heart of intense situations where split-second decisions can mean the difference between life and death.

Navigating the Negotiation Landscape:

In this Wall Street Journal Bestseller, Voss shares the wealth of experience gained from facing criminals ranging from bank robbers to terrorists. The principles and strategies outlined in "Never Split the Difference" extend far beyond the confines of law enforcement. Whether you're in the boardroom, making major life decisions, or navigating everyday transactions, this workbook is your guide to mastering the art of negotiation.

Insider's Access to Tactical Wisdom:

Gain exclusive access to Voss's mindset as he unravels the intricate dance of high-stakes negotiations. This workbook transforms the theoretical into the practical, offering you hands-on activities, thought-provoking exercises, and real-world scenarios to hone your negotiation skills.

Unveiling the Nine Effective Principles:

Discover the counterintuitive tactics and strategies that have proven successful in the most challenging circumstances. From mirroring to tactical empathy, each principle is a powerful tool you can wield to become more persuasive, more influential, and ultimately, more successful in both your professional and personal life.

Prepare for Life's Negotiations:

Life is a continuous negotiation, from purchasing a car to navigating the complexities of personal relationships. This workbook takes the principles outlined in "Never Split the Difference" and guides you in applying them to the myriad negotiations life throws your way.

Empower Yourself with Emotional Intelligence:

Elevate your negotiation game by taking emotional intelligence and intuition to the next level. As you delve into the interactive exercises and reflective questions within these pages, you'll not only absorb Voss's teachings but also develop the skills needed to gain a competitive edge in any discussion.

Embark on this transformative journey through the world of high-stakes negotiations, armed with the knowledge and practical application that will empower you to navigate life's negotiations with confidence and skill. Let's delve into the principles that can reshape the way you approach every interaction, ensuring you never split the difference again.

THE NEW RULE

SUMMARY

Chapter One of "Never Split the Difference" introduces the concept of "The New Rule," emphasizing the shift from traditional negotiation approaches to a more empathetic and tactical mindset. Chris Voss, drawing on his experience as an FBI hostage negotiator, challenges the idea that rational decision-making solely drives negotiations. Instead, he advocates for understanding and influencing the emotional drivers behind decisions.

Key Lessons:
- Tactical Empathy: The chapter underscores the importance of tactical empathy, where negotiators seek to understand the emotions and perspectives of the other party. This approach fosters a stronger connection and opens the door for more effective communication.

- Emotional Intelligence: Voss emphasizes the need for heightened emotional intelligence in negotiations. Recognizing and addressing emotions, both your own and the other party's, is crucial for successful outcomes.

- Dynamic Communication: Negotiation is portrayed as a dynamic, evolving process where adaptability and responsiveness to the other party's cues play a central role. The chapter challenges the idea that negotiations are linear and rational transactions.

INTERACTIVE QUESTIONS

RECALL A NEGOTIATION FROM YOUR PERSONAL OR PROFESSIONAL LIFE.

WHAT EMOTIONS WERE AT PLAY, AND HOW MIGHT THE APPLICATION OF TACTICAL EMPATHY HAVE INFLUENCED THE OUTCOME?

_____

_____

_____

_____

_____

_____

THINK ABOUT A NEGOTIATION WHERE COMMUNICATION BREAKDOWNS OCCURRED.

HOW MIGHT A MORE DYNAMIC AND ADAPTABLE COMMUNICATION STYLE, AS DISCUSSED IN CHAPTER ONE, HAVE IMPROVED THE INTERACTION?

BE A MIRROR

SUMMARY

Chapter Two delves into the powerful technique of mirroring. Chris Voss introduces the concept of mirroring as a method of building rapport and establishing a connection with the other party. Mirroring involves repeating the last few words or a key phrase spoken by the counterpart, creating a subconscious bond and fostering a sense of understanding. Voss emphasizes the effectiveness of mirroring in diffusing tension and encouraging open communication.

Key Lessons:

- Building Rapport: Mirroring is a tool for building rapport by demonstrating active listening. By reflecting the counterpart's words, negotiators signal empathy and understanding, establishing a foundation for trust.

- Creating a Connection: Mirroring helps create a psychological bond. It encourages the counterpart to feel heard and validated, contributing to a more collaborative and cooperative negotiation environment.

- Encouraging Openness: Mirroring invites the other party to share more information. The technique often prompts counterparts to elaborate on their thoughts and feelings, providing valuable insights for the negotiator.

INTERACTIVE QUESTIONS

CHOOSE A CONVERSATION IN YOUR PERSONAL OR PROFESSIONAL LIFE TO PRACTICE MIRRORING.

☐ USEFUL

☐ NOT USEFUL

REFLECT ON HOW MIRRORING INFLUENCED THE DYNAMICS OF THE CONVERSATION AND WHETHER IT LED TO A DEEPER CONNECTION.

_____

_____

_____

_____

_____

COMPARE THE OUTCOMES AND COMMUNICATION DYNAMICS OF THOSE SITUATIONS WITH THE POTENTIAL IMPACT OF INCORPORATING MIRRORING. WHAT DIFFERENCES DO YOU OBSERVE?

_____

_____

_____

_____

_____

_____

_____

_____

DON'T FEEL THEIR PAIN, LABEL IT

SUMMARY

Chapter Three introduces the concept of labeling emotions as a powerful tool in negotiation. Chris Voss emphasizes the importance of acknowledging and labeling the emotions of both parties to create a bridge for understanding. Instead of directly empathizing or sympathizing, labeling involves verbalizing and validating the other party's feelings. This chapter explores how labeling can deescalate tension, build trust, and pave the way for more productive conversations.

Key Lessons:
- Emotional Acknowledgment: Rather than avoiding or dismissing emotions, successful negotiators acknowledge and label them. This not only demonstrates empathy but also helps in defusing potential conflicts.

- Creating a Sense of Control: Labeling empowers negotiators by providing a structured way to address emotions. It allows the negotiator to assert control over the emotional atmosphere of the negotiation.

- Building Trust through Validation: By labeling the other party's emotions, negotiators show that they understand and validate those feelings. This fosters a sense of trust and openness, contributing to a more collaborative negotiation process.

INTERACTIVE QUESTIONS

RECALL A NEGOTIATION WHERE EMOTIONS WERE EVIDENT.

PRACTICE LABELING BY IDENTIFYING AND VERBALIZING THE EMOTIONS EXPRESSED BY BOTH PARTIES. REFLECT ON HOW THIS IMPACTED THE NEGOTIATION DYNAMICS.

REFLECT ON A NEGOTIATION WHERE TRUST PLAYED A CRUCIAL ROLE.

HOW MIGHT THE USE OF LABELING HAVE CONTRIBUTED TO BUILDING OR REINFORCING TRUST IN THAT SITUATION? CONSIDER SPECIFIC EXAMPLES.

_____

_____

_____

_____

_____

_____

BEWARE "YES"- MASTER "NO"

SUMMARY

In Chapter Four, Chris Voss explores the dynamics of affirmatives and negatives in negotiation. Voss challenges the common belief that "yes" is always the desired response, emphasizing the power of "no" as a strategic tool. The chapter introduces the concept of the "no-oriented question" and how it can be used to gather valuable information, build rapport, and guide the negotiation process.

Key Lessons:

- The Power of "No": "No" is not the end of negotiation but a gateway to deeper understanding and collaboration. It allows negotiators to explore concerns, identify obstacles, and create solutions that address the underlying issues.

- Using "No" as Protection: "No" can be a protective response, signaling caution or a need for more information. Skilled negotiators use this as an opportunity to uncover concerns, build trust, and guide the conversation towards mutually beneficial outcomes.

- Crafting "No-Oriented" Questions: The chapter emphasizes the art of crafting questions that naturally lead to a "no" response. This technique encourages open communication, as individuals often feel more comfortable expressing their true thoughts and concerns when given permission to say "no."

INTERACTIVE QUESTIONS

REFLECT ON YOUR PAST REACTIONS TO HEARING "NO" IN NEGOTIATIONS.

HOW HAS YOUR PERCEPTION OF THIS RESPONSE EVOLVED, AND HOW MIGHT EMBRACING "NO" POSITIVELY IMPACT YOUR NEGOTIATION APPROACH?

RECALL A NEGOTIATION WHERE YOU RECEIVED A "NO" RESPONSE.

REFLECT ON HOW THAT MOMENT INFLUENCED THE SUBSEQUENT NEGOTIATION AND EXPLORE POTENTIAL STRATEGIES FOR TURNING THAT "NO" INTO A POSITIVE OUTCOME.

_____

_____

_____

_____

_____

_____

TRIGGER THE TWO WORDS THAT IMMEDIATELY TRANSFORM ANY NEGOTIATION

SUMMARY

In Chapter Five, Chris Voss explores the transformative power of the phrase "That's Right." This chapter introduces the concept of tactical empathy and the profound impact of getting the counterpart to acknowledge your understanding. "That's Right" becomes a crucial tool in achieving this acknowledgment, creating a moment of alignment that enhances rapport, understanding, and cooperation.

Key Lessons:

- Tactical Empathy: Acknowledging and understanding the counterpart's perspective is at the heart of tactical empathy. The phrase "That's Right" serves as a powerful confirmation that you grasp the other party's feelings and thoughts.

- Building Rapport Through Agreement: Getting the counterpart to say "That's Right" is a moment of agreement that transcends a simple acknowledgment. It fosters a sense of connection and aligns both parties towards a common understanding.

- Creating a Collaborative Atmosphere: The chapter emphasizes the role of "That's Right" in transforming the negotiation atmosphere into one of collaboration. It sets the stage for problem-solving and reaching mutually beneficial agreements.

INTERACTIVE QUESTIONS

REFLECT ON INSTANCES WHERE THE COUNTERPART ACKNOWLEDGED YOUR UNDERSTANDING.

HOW DID THIS IMPACT THE NEGOTIATION, AND WHAT COULD BE REPLICATED IN FUTURE INTERACTIONS?

_____

_____

_____

_____

_____

_____

REFLECT ON A NEGOTIATION WHERE MUTUAL AGREEMENT WAS A TURNING POINT.

HOW DID THE ATMOSPHERE CHANGE WHEN BOTH PARTIES FOUND COMMON GROUND? CONSIDER HOW THE ACKNOWLEDGMENT OF SHARED UNDERSTANDING INFLUENCED THE NEGOTIATION TRAJECTORY.

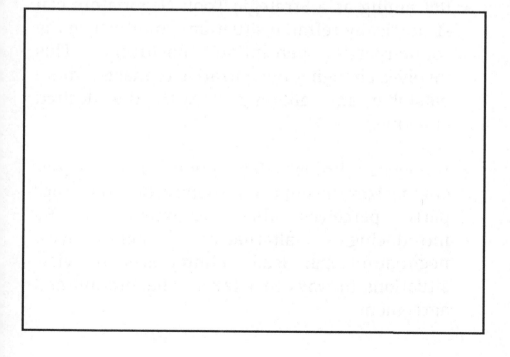

BEND THEIR REALITY

SUMMARY

In Chapter Six, Chris Voss explores the concept of reframing and the power of influencing the counterpart's perception. The chapter delves into the idea that altering the way the other party views a situation can lead to more favorable outcomes. By using tactical empathy and strategic communication, negotiators can reshape their counterpart's reality and guide them towards mutually beneficial agreements.

Key Lessons:

- Reframing as a Strategic Tool: Negotiators can strategically reframe situations to influence the counterpart's perception positively. This involves changing the narrative to make it more palatable and aligning it with the desired outcome.

- Influence through Perception: The chapter emphasizes the impact of shaping how the other party perceives their circumstances. By introducing alternative perspectives, negotiators can lead counterparts to view situations in ways that favor collaboration and agreement.

- Leveraging Tactical Empathy: Reframing is closely tied to tactical empathy. Understanding the emotions and concerns of the counterpart allows negotiators to tailor their communication in a way that bends the reality in a direction conducive to successful negotiations.

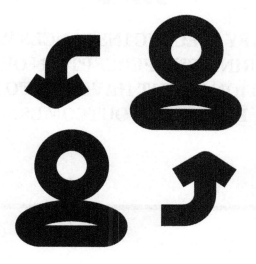

INTERACTIVE QUESTIONS

REFLECT ON PAST NEGOTIATIONS WHERE
REFRAMING COULD HAVE BEEN BENEFICIAL.

IDENTIFY SPECIFIC INSTANCES WHERE
ALTERING THE PERCEPTION OF THE
SITUATION MIGHT HAVE LED TO MORE
FAVORABLE OUTCOMES.

○ _____

○ _____

○ _____

○ _____

RECALL NEGOTIATIONS WHERE YOU SUCCESSFULLY REFRAMED A SITUATION.

WHAT WAS THE CONTEXT, AND HOW DID THE REFRAMING INFLUENCE THE COUNTERPART'S RESPONSE? EXPLORE WAYS TO REPLICATE THESE SUCCESSES IN FUTURE NEGOTIATIONS.

CREATE THE ILLUSION OF CONTROL

SUMMARY

In Chapter Seven, Chris Voss introduces the concept of allowing the counterpart to feel in control while guiding the negotiation process. The chapter explores the psychology of control and how negotiators can strategically influence the other party's perception to foster cooperation. By offering choices and alternatives within controlled parameters, negotiators create a sense of empowerment for the counterpart, leading to more successful outcomes.

Key Lessons:
- Illusion of Control: Negotiators can influence the counterpart's behavior by allowing them to feel a sense of control over the situation. This psychological strategy involves guiding the negotiation while giving the other party the impression that they are making decisions.

- Navigating Resistance: Creating the illusion of control is particularly effective in navigating resistance. By providing options and framing choices, negotiators can overcome objections and guide the counterpart towards agreement.

- Strategic Empowerment: The chapter emphasizes the strategic empowerment of the counterpart. Negotiators achieve this by offering choices that align with their goals while ensuring that the overall negotiation remains within desired parameters.

INTERACTIVE QUESTIONS

REFLECT ON INSTANCES WHERE THE ILLUSION OF CONTROL COULD HAVE BEEN EMPLOYED TO NAVIGATE CHALLENGES AND FOSTER COLLABORATION.

_____

_____

_____

_____

_____

_____

_____

_____

_____

_____

RECALL NEGOTIATIONS WHERE THE COUNTERPART FELT EMPOWERED.

HOW DID THIS INFLUENCE THE OVERALL NEGOTIATION ATMOSPHERE, AND WHAT WERE THE OUTCOMES? CONSIDER WAYS TO REPLICATE THESE EMPOWERING MOMENTS IN FUTURE NEGOTIATIONS.

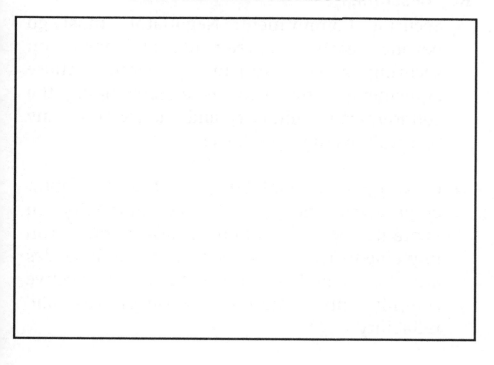

GUARANTEE EXECUTION

SUMMARY

In Chapter Eight, Chris Voss explores the importance of ensuring that agreements are not only made but also executed. The chapter delves into the psychology of commitment and how negotiators can secure a commitment from the counterpart to follow through on agreed-upon terms. By addressing potential pitfalls and incorporating accountability measures, negotiators can enhance the likelihood of successful execution of agreements.

Key Lessons:

- Securing Commitment: Negotiators must go beyond reaching agreements and focus on securing a commitment to execute those agreements. This involves understanding the counterpart's mindset and addressing any reservations they may have.

- Creating Accountability: The chapter emphasizes the role of accountability in guaranteeing execution. Negotiators can implement strategies to ensure that both parties are accountable for their respective commitments, fostering a sense of trust and reliability.

- Navigating Implementation Challenges: Negotiators need to anticipate and address potential challenges in the execution phase. By proactively addressing concerns and maintaining open communication, they increase the likelihood of successful implementation.

INTERACTIVE QUESTIONS

REFLECT ON INSTANCES WHERE EXECUTION
FELL SHORT. WHAT WERE THE CONTRIBUTING
FACTORS, AND HOW MIGHT THE STRATEGIES
FROM CHAPTER EIGHT HAVE ADDRESSED
THOSE CHALLENGES?

_____

_____

_____

_____

_____

_____

_____

_____

_____

RECALL NEGOTIATIONS WHERE EXECUTION WAS PARTICULARLY SUCCESSFUL.

WHAT FACTORS CONTRIBUTED TO THE SMOOTH IMPLEMENTATION, AND HOW CAN YOU APPLY THOSE LESSONS TO FUTURE NEGOTIATIONS? CONSIDER SPECIFIC ACTIONS THAT LED TO POSITIVE OUTCOMES.

BARGAIN HARD

SUMMARY

In Chapter Nine, Chris Voss explores the art of effective bargaining in negotiations. The chapter delves into the tactics and mindset needed to navigate the give-and-take of bargaining, emphasizing the importance of patience, strategic concessions, and maintaining a strong position. Voss provides insights into handling the pressure of bargaining situations and achieving outcomes that align with negotiators' goals.

Key Lessons:

- Strategic Concessions: Effective bargaining involves making strategic concessions to build rapport and foster a collaborative atmosphere. Negotiators must carefully consider when and how to concede without compromising their overall objectives.

- Maintaining Assertiveness: Bargaining requires a balance between assertiveness and flexibility. Negotiators should stand firm on crucial points while remaining open to opportunities for compromise that advance the negotiation toward a mutually beneficial outcome.

- Patience in Bargaining: The chapter emphasizes the need for patience in the bargaining process. Negotiators should resist the urge to rush decisions and instead allow the negotiation to unfold, creating space for more favorable concessions.

INTERACTIVE QUESTIONS

REFLECT ON INSTANCES WHERE STRATEGIC CONCESSIONS WERE EFFECTIVE AND TIMES WHEN MAINTAINING ASSERTIVENESS LED TO POSITIVE OUTCOMES.

_____

_____

_____

_____

_____

_____

_____

_____

_____

DEVELOP A STRATEGY FOR MAINTAINING PATIENCE AND RESISTING THE PRESSURE TO RUSH DECISIONS. CONSIDER HOW THIS APPROACH MIGHT INFLUENCE THE BARGAINING DYNAMICS.

FIND THE BLACK SWAN

SUMMARY

In Chapter Ten, Chris Voss discusses the importance of identifying unexpected or hidden factors that can significantly impact negotiations. The chapter introduces the concept of the "Black Swan," an unforeseen event or piece of information that can change the entire dynamics of a negotiation. Voss emphasizes the need for vigilance, adaptability, and continuous information gathering to anticipate and navigate these unforeseen challenges effectively.

Key Lessons:

- Anticipating Unforeseen Challenges: Negotiators must be proactive in identifying potential Black Swan events that could disrupt the negotiation process. This requires a mindset of continuous awareness and a willingness to adapt to changing circumstances.

- Adaptability as a Key Skill: The chapter underscores the importance of adaptability in the face of unexpected developments. Skilled negotiators are prepared to pivot their strategies and adjust their approach when confronted with unforeseen challenges.

- Continuous Information Gathering: Negotiators should prioritize ongoing information gathering throughout the negotiation. This involves actively seeking out new insights, staying attuned to changes in the environment, and being receptive to unexpected information that may emerge.

INTERACTIVE QUESTIONS

RECALL NEGOTIATIONS WHERE UNEXPECTED
EVENTS HAD A SIGNIFICANT IMPACT.

REFLECT ON HOW THESE EVENTS WERE
HANDLED AND CONSIDER STRATEGIES THAT
COULD HAVE HELPED ANTICIPATE OR
NAVIGATE THEM MORE EFFECTIVELY.

DEVELOP A PLAN TO ENHANCE YOUR ABILITY TO CONTINUOUSLY GATHER RELEVANT INFORMATION, ANTICIPATE POTENTIAL BLACK SWAN EVENTS, AND ADJUST YOUR STRATEGY ACCORDINGLY.

_____

_____

_____

_____

_____

_____

_____

_____

_____

_____

CONCLUSION

In conclusion, "Never Split the Difference" by Chris Voss is a compelling guide that unlocks the secrets of effective negotiation, drawing on Voss's experience as an FBI hostage negotiator. The book presents a holistic approach to negotiations, emphasizing emotional intelligence, tactical empathy, and strategic communication. As we've explored key chapters, each one has contributed valuable insights and lessons to enhance negotiation skills.

- Tactical Empathy and Mirroring: Chapters Two and Three introduce tactical empathy and mirroring as powerful tools. Understanding and reflecting on the emotions of the counterpart build rapport and create a foundation for successful negotiations.

- Labeling and Reframing: Chapters Four and Six delve into the art of labeling emotions and reframing situations. These techniques provide negotiators with the ability to navigate emotional landscapes and influence perceptions positively.

- Empowerment and Control: Chapters Seven and Eight discuss creating the illusion of control and guaranteeing execution. Negotiators learn to strategically empower counterparts while ensuring commitments are honored, fostering a sense of reliability and trust.

- Bargaining and Adaptability: In Chapter Nine, bargaining strategies are explored, emphasizing the delicate balance between assertiveness and flexibility. Chapter Ten encourages negotiators to anticipate and adapt to unforeseen challenges, embodying the concept of finding the Black Swan.

Interactive Workbook Integration:

The provided workbook prompts offer a hands-on approach to applying these principles. From practicing mirroring to simulating Black Swan scenarios, the workbook facilitates active engagement, helping negotiators internalize concepts and enhance their skills.

Continuous Growth:

Negotiation is an evolving skill, and "Never Split the Difference" provides timeless principles for success. Whether navigating emotions, securing commitments, or adapting to unexpected events, negotiators equipped with these insights can approach negotiations with confidence and finesse.

As you embark on your journey to master the art of negotiation, remember that each negotiation is a unique opportunity to refine and apply these principles. With empathy, adaptability, and strategic thinking, you can navigate negotiations successfully, securing outcomes that benefit all parties involved.

PERSONAL NOTES